Calm
Confident
Capable

A daily journal to get you out of your
head and into your heart

By: Kelsey Dalziel

.

About the journal

Hello reader!

If you're anything like me you feel like you have a million things on the go. I am a busy mom of 3, wife, CEO of my Spiritual Medium and a Soul Coaching business, cook, cleaner, household management etc, etc.

Your life may differ in many ways but one thing we may agree on is balance is a myth and overwhelm is real.

As I started to build my business, fear of unworthiness started to creep into my head. I would feel stuck and spin my tires until I hit burnout - exhausted and unable to show up in the ways I was needed to show up.

As I worked with more clients - mainly women, similar patterns would show up in their lives. Lack, overwhelm, insecurity and longing for something more. Certain teachings that came through me intuitively started repeating themselves. I started implementing these practices in my own life - mainly in my morning journaling practice.

One night as I was trying to fall asleep, inspiration struck - What if I put my top 6 teachings into a daily practice that myself and others could use?

And so it is!

My intention in sharing this journal with you is to introduce a simple daily ritual that will keep you Calm, teach you Confidence and show you how Capable you are of transforming your life into one you can love fully. The following pages will explain to you the process and the WHY behind each practice.

Big Love,

Kelsey

CALM

Seven years ago I was in a pretty bad place. I was a stay at home mom, work at home mom, cry at home mom. I was depressed, and stuck wondering if I'd made the right choices in life. I had a moment where i asked the "something bigger than us" that I now call the Universe, (you may call it God or the Creator) for help. I was in total surrender because the anxiety and sadness that held me down every day was just too much ..... After a series of synchronistic events, I found myself trained as a Meditation Teacher.

That world led me to travel to the US and train with a well known spiritual teacher and literally change my life in ways I couldn't imagine. Today I use meditation as a baseline for all things. Frustrated? Did I meditate today? Overwhelmed? Did I meditate today? Stuck? Did I meditate today? When used as a daily tool, meditation becomes as natural and essential as brushing your teeth. I teach all of my students and clients the benefits of meditation because it supports us physically, mentally emotionally and spiritually. Meditation not only gives us a safe space to land and an opportunity to check in (or check out) but it actually changes our brains. It creates neural pathways (think shortcuts!) to a sense of calm, builds resilience, and helps us access more responsive, rational thought patterns.

If you have a meditation practice already, please implement it in your daily practice first thing when you wake up, followed by the exercises in this journal. If you are new to meditation I invite you to access the guided meditation that I have created for this practice here –

https://vimeo.com/342782418/83e119195a

CONFIDENT

The confidence portion consists of 2 exercises.

The first is a simple list of 5 things you are grateful for. Gratitude makes what we have enough and the practice of it literally trains our brains to operate from the perspective of abundance instead of the lack mindset that holds us back from living fully. When we focus on the things we have with appreciation, we unblock the flow of giving and receiving that the universe is here to support us with. It is important to not just ''think about things we are grateful for but FEEL the emotion as well. At all times you are sending signals through your energy to the world around you. This vibration is matched and reflected back to you from the Universe. If you simply make a quick list of things you're grateful for, it's just a list. If you take the time to get to the WHY, you can get into the vibration of gratitude quicker and deeper and become a magnetic match for more.

The second exercise was given to me from the universe one day as I sat in my car and witnessed my head swirling with thoughts I recognized to be completely untrue. I observed negative thoughts like, 'you're not smart enough for success', 'nobody cares what you have to say, you look like a fool.' I knew them to be untrue because I had seen these exact narratives in a client the day before and coached her to tune into her heart for the truth. I did the same for myself, placed my hands on my heart, took a deep breath and listened. "You are more than smart enough and you are already successful. You are teaching people to follow their dreams simply by following theirs. People are listening and the ripple effect is there even when you can't see it.' My exercise known as 'head says/heart says' has been one of the most powerful practices I use in my own life and with my clients. It takes me from pessimism to optimism, fear to love in mere seconds.

CAPABLE

The practice of visualization has always been popular in personal and spiritual development circles but recently it has been discovered that practicing being in the emotion of already having what you desire is much more effective in manifestation. When you write down your desires as if they have already happened, you are telling the universe you already have it and are grateful for it - The Universe is like a mirror and gives you back exactly what you project.

The first exercise in this section is writing down what you would like to accomplish. It can be anything from organizing your cupboards to publishing a book. Maybe it's taking a dream vacation or breaking a bad habit. Making the statement 'I am completely capable of _____' is powerful on its own, but pairing it with the next exercise is where the real magic happens

The second exercise is called Future Tense Freewrite. This exercise is truly powerful because writing as if what you want is already done not only helps you shake out what you REALLY want but helps bring it to you through gratitude. Remember energy is energy and whether negative or positive the Universe doesn't care if it's real or not - it simply reflects back to you what you put out. In this exercise write as if you are reflecting back on the past week, month and year. Let yourself get into it and don't hold back!

EXAMPLE

Week: *"I'm so happy I took the time to relax this week. My plate was definitely FULL. Once I made a to-do list I was able to get everything done. The surprise party I planned for my sister was AWESOME! Everyone had a great time and it was great to see everyone again!"*

Month: *"I remember a month ago when I was chatting with friends about a business idea. I can't get the idea out of my head and am making calls to people who I think can help. I've always wanted to work for myself and I feel like this is the right time. Everything is falling to place and I can't wait to see where this goes!"*

Year: *"I remember a year ago when I started thinking about starting a business and I'm actually doing it. Everything seemed to fall into place so easily. I'm really glad I listened to my intuition. I have the freedom to spend more time with my family and we are looking forward to Maui next week. By spending more time working from home we were finally able to get a dog and he is such a blessing! The kids are really helping out and they are so happy to have me home. I really feel like I've found my groove. Life is beautiful!"*

Calm

Confident

Capable

Date____/____

Today I feel deep gratitude for _____because
_____

Today I feel deep gratitude for _____because
_____

Today I feel deep gratitude for _____because
_____

Today I feel deep gratitude for _____because
_____

Today I feel deep gratitude for _____because
_____

Today my head says:
_____
_____
_____

But my heart says:
_____
_____
_____

I am completely capable of:

1_____
2_____
3_____

Future tense freewrite:

One week _____

_____

_____

_____

_____

_____

_____

_____

_____

_____

One month _____

_____

_____

_____

_____

_____

_____

_____

_____

_____

One year _____

_____

_____

_____

_____

_____

_____

_____

_____

_____

Date____/____

Today I feel deep gratitude for _____because
_____

Today I feel deep gratitude for _____because
_____

Today I feel deep gratitude for _____because
_____

Today I feel deep gratitude for _____because
_____

Today I feel deep gratitude for _____because
_____

Today my head says:
_____
_____
_____

But my heart says:
_____
_____
_____

I am completely capable of:

1_____
2_____
3_____

Future tense freewrite:

One week _____

_____
_____
_____
_____
_____
_____
_____
_____
_____

One month _____

_____
_____
_____
_____
_____
_____
_____
_____
_____

One year _____

_____
_____
_____
_____
_____
_____
_____
_____
_____

Date_____/_____

Today I feel deep gratitude for _____because
_____

Today I feel deep gratitude for _____because
_____

Today I feel deep gratitude for _____because
_____

Today I feel deep gratitude for _____because
_____

Today I feel deep gratitude for _____because
_____

Today my head says:
_____
_____
_____

But my heart says:
_____
_____
_____

I am completely capable of:

1_____
2_____
3_____

Future tense freewrite:

One week _____
_____
_____
_____
_____
_____
_____
_____
_____
_____

One month _____
_____
_____
_____
_____
_____
_____
_____
_____
_____

One year _____
_____
_____
_____
_____
_____
_____
_____
_____

Date____/____

Today I feel deep gratitude for _____because
_____

Today I feel deep gratitude for _____because
_____

Today I feel deep gratitude for _____because
_____

Today I feel deep gratitude for _____because
_____

Today I feel deep gratitude for _____because
_____

Today my head says:
_____
_____
_____

But my heart says:
_____
_____
_____

I am completely capable of:

1_____
2_____
3_____

Future tense freewrite:

One week _____

_____

_____

_____

_____

_____

_____

_____

_____

_____

One month _____

_____

_____

_____

_____

_____

_____

_____

_____

_____

One year _____

_____

_____

_____

_____

_____

_____

_____

_____

_____

Date____/____

Today I feel deep gratitude for _____because
_____

Today I feel deep gratitude for _____because
_____

Today I feel deep gratitude for _____because
_____

Today I feel deep gratitude for _____because
_____

Today I feel deep gratitude for _____because
_____

Today my head says:
_____
_____
_____

But my heart says:
_____
_____
_____

I am completely capable of:

1_____
2_____
3_____

Future tense freewrite:

One week _____

_____
_____
_____
_____
_____
_____
_____
_____
_____

One month _____

_____
_____
_____
_____
_____
_____
_____
_____
_____
_____

One year _____

_____
_____
_____
_____
_____
_____
_____
_____
_____
_____

Date____/____

Today I feel deep gratitude for _____because
_____

Today I feel deep gratitude for _____because
_____

Today I feel deep gratitude for _____because
_____

Today I feel deep gratitude for _____because
_____

Today I feel deep gratitude for _____because
_____

Today my head says:
_____
_____
_____

But my heart says:
_____
_____
_____

I am completely capable of:

1_____
2_____
3_____

Future tense freewrite:

One week _____

_____

_____

_____

_____

_____

_____

_____

_____

_____

One month _____

_____

_____

_____

_____

_____

_____

_____

_____

_____

One year _____

_____

_____

_____

_____

_____

_____

_____

_____

_____

Date____/____

Today I feel deep gratitude for _____because
_____

Today I feel deep gratitude for _____because
_____

Today I feel deep gratitude for _____because
_____

Today I feel deep gratitude for _____because
_____

Today I feel deep gratitude for _____because
_____

Today my head says:
_____
_____
_____

But my heart says:
_____
_____
_____

I am completely capable of:

1_____
2_____
3_____

Future tense freewrite:

One week _____
_____
_____
_____
_____
_____
_____
_____
_____
_____

One month _____
_____
_____
_____
_____
_____
_____
_____
_____
_____

One year _____
_____
_____
_____
_____
_____
_____
_____
_____
_____

Date____/____

Today I feel deep gratitude for _____because
_____

Today I feel deep gratitude for _____because
_____

Today I feel deep gratitude for _____because
_____

Today I feel deep gratitude for _____because
_____

Today I feel deep gratitude for _____because
_____

Today my head says:
_____
_____
_____

But my heart says:
_____
_____
_____

I am completely capable of:

1_____
2_____
3_____

Future tense freewrite:

One week _____

_____

_____

_____

_____

_____

_____

_____

_____

_____

One month _____

_____

_____

_____

_____

_____

_____

_____

_____

_____

One year _____

_____

_____

_____

_____

_____

_____

_____

_____

_____

Date____/____

Today I feel deep gratitude for _____because
_____

Today I feel deep gratitude for _____because
_____

Today I feel deep gratitude for _____because
_____

Today I feel deep gratitude for _____because
_____

Today I feel deep gratitude for _____because
_____

Today my head says:
_____
_____
_____

But my heart says:
_____
_____
_____

I am completely capable of:

1_____
2_____
3_____

Future tense freewrite:

One week _____
_____
_____
_____
_____
_____
_____
_____
_____
_____

One month _____
_____
_____
_____
_____
_____
_____
_____
_____
_____

One year _____
_____
_____
_____
_____
_____
_____
_____
_____

Date____/____

Today I feel deep gratitude for _____because
_____

Today I feel deep gratitude for _____because
_____

Today I feel deep gratitude for _____because
_____

Today I feel deep gratitude for _____because
_____

Today I feel deep gratitude for _____because
_____

Today my head says:
_____
_____
_____

But my heart says:
_____
_____
_____

I am completely capable of:

1_____
2_____
3_____

Future tense freewrite:

One week _____
_____
_____
_____
_____
_____
_____
_____
_____
_____

One month _____
_____
_____
_____
_____
_____
_____
_____
_____
_____

One year _____
_____
_____
_____
_____
_____
_____
_____
_____
_____

Date____/____

Today I feel deep gratitude for _____because
_____

Today I feel deep gratitude for _____because
_____

Today I feel deep gratitude for _____because
_____

Today I feel deep gratitude for _____because
_____

Today I feel deep gratitude for _____because
_____

Today my head says:
_____
_____
_____

But my heart says:
_____
_____
_____

I am completely capable of:

1_____
2_____
3_____

Future tense freewrite:

One week _____

_____

_____

_____

_____

_____

_____

_____

_____

_____

One month _____

_____

_____

_____

_____

_____

_____

_____

_____

_____

One year _____

_____

_____

_____

_____

_____

_____

_____

_____

_____

Date____/____

Today I feel deep gratitude for _____because
_____

Today I feel deep gratitude for _____because
_____

Today I feel deep gratitude for _____because
_____

Today I feel deep gratitude for _____because
_____

Today I feel deep gratitude for _____because
_____

Today my head says:
_____
_____
_____

But my heart says:
_____
_____
_____

I am completely capable of:

1_____
2_____
3_____

Future tense freewrite:

One week _____

_____

_____

_____

_____

_____

_____

_____

_____

_____

One month _____

_____

_____

_____

_____

_____

_____

_____

_____

_____

One year _____

_____

_____

_____

_____

_____

_____

_____

_____

_____

Date____/____

Today I feel deep gratitude for _____because
_____

Today I feel deep gratitude for _____because
_____

Today I feel deep gratitude for _____because
_____

Today I feel deep gratitude for _____because
_____

Today I feel deep gratitude for _____because
_____

Today my head says:
_____
_____
_____

But my heart says:
_____
_____
_____

I am completely capable of:

1_____
2_____
3_____

Future tense freewrite:

One week _____
_____
_____
_____
_____
_____
_____
_____
_____
_____

One month _____
_____
_____
_____
_____
_____
_____
_____
_____
_____

One year _____
_____
_____
_____
_____
_____
_____
_____
_____
_____

Date____/____

Today I feel deep gratitude for _____because
_____

Today I feel deep gratitude for _____because
_____

Today I feel deep gratitude for _____because
_____

Today I feel deep gratitude for _____because
_____

Today I feel deep gratitude for _____because
_____

Today my head says:
_____
_____
_____

But my heart says:
_____
_____
_____

I am completely capable of:

1_____
2_____
3_____

Future tense freewrite:

One week _____

_____

_____

_____

_____

_____

_____

_____

_____

_____

One month _____

_____

_____

_____

_____

_____

_____

_____

_____

_____

One year _____

_____

_____

_____

_____

_____

_____

_____

_____

_____

Date____/____

Today I feel deep gratitude for _____because
_____

Today I feel deep gratitude for _____because
_____

Today I feel deep gratitude for _____because
_____

Today I feel deep gratitude for _____because
_____

Today I feel deep gratitude for _____because
_____

Today my head says:
_____
_____
_____

But my heart says:
_____
_____
_____

I am completely capable of:

1_____
2_____
3_____

Future tense freewrite:

One week _____

_____
_____
_____
_____
_____
_____
_____
_____
_____

One month _____

_____
_____
_____
_____
_____
_____
_____
_____
_____

One year _____

_____
_____
_____
_____
_____
_____
_____
_____

Date____/____

Today I feel deep gratitude for _____because
_____

Today I feel deep gratitude for _____because
_____

Today I feel deep gratitude for _____because
_____

Today I feel deep gratitude for _____because
_____

Today I feel deep gratitude for _____because
_____

Today my head says:
_____
_____
_____

But my heart says:
_____
_____
_____

I am completely capable of:

1_____
2_____
3_____

Future tense freewrite:

One week _____

_____
_____
_____
_____
_____
_____
_____
_____
_____

One month _____

_____
_____
_____
_____
_____
_____
_____
_____
_____

One year _____

_____
_____
_____
_____
_____
_____
_____
_____
_____

Date____/____

Today I feel deep gratitude for _____because
_____

Today I feel deep gratitude for _____because
_____

Today I feel deep gratitude for _____because
_____

Today I feel deep gratitude for _____because
_____

Today I feel deep gratitude for _____because
_____

Today my head says:
_____
_____
_____

But my heart says:
_____
_____
_____

I am completely capable of:

1_____
2_____
3_____

Future tense freewrite:

One week _____

_____
_____
_____
_____
_____
_____
_____
_____
_____
_____

One month _____

_____
_____
_____
_____
_____
_____
_____
_____
_____
_____

One year _____

_____
_____
_____
_____
_____
_____
_____
_____
_____
_____

Date_____/_____

Today I feel deep gratitude for _____because
_____

Today I feel deep gratitude for _____because
_____

Today I feel deep gratitude for _____because
_____

Today I feel deep gratitude for _____because
_____

Today I feel deep gratitude for _____because
_____

Today my head says:
_____
_____
_____

But my heart says:
_____
_____
_____

I am completely capable of:

1_____
2_____
3_____

Future tense freewrite:

One week _____

_____

_____

_____

_____

_____

_____

_____

_____

_____

One month _____

_____

_____

_____

_____

_____

_____

_____

_____

_____

One year _____

_____

_____

_____

_____

_____

_____

_____

_____

_____

Date____/____

Today I feel deep gratitude for _____because
_____

Today I feel deep gratitude for _____because
_____

Today I feel deep gratitude for _____because
_____

Today I feel deep gratitude for _____because
_____

Today I feel deep gratitude for _____because
_____

Today my head says:
_____
_____
_____

But my heart says:
_____
_____
_____

I am completely capable of:

1_____
2_____
3_____

Future tense freewrite:

One week _____

_____
_____
_____
_____
_____
_____
_____
_____
_____

One month _____

_____
_____
_____
_____
_____
_____
_____
_____
_____
_____

One year _____

_____
_____
_____
_____
_____
_____
_____
_____
_____
_____

Date____/____

Today I feel deep gratitude for _____because
_____

Today I feel deep gratitude for _____because
_____

Today I feel deep gratitude for _____because
_____

Today I feel deep gratitude for _____because
_____

Today I feel deep gratitude for _____because
_____

Today my head says:
_____
_____
_____

But my heart says:
_____
_____
_____

I am completely capable of:

1_____
2_____
3_____

Future tense freewrite:

One week _____

_____

_____

_____

_____

_____

_____

_____

_____

_____

One month _____

_____

_____

_____

_____

_____

_____

_____

_____

_____

One year _____

_____

_____

_____

_____

_____

_____

_____

_____

_____

Date____/____

Today I feel deep gratitude for _____because
_____

Today I feel deep gratitude for _____because
_____

Today I feel deep gratitude for _____because
_____

Today I feel deep gratitude for _____because
_____

Today I feel deep gratitude for _____because
_____

Today my head says:
_____
_____
_____

But my heart says:
_____
_____
_____

I am completely capable of:

1_____
2_____
3_____

Future tense freewrite:

One week _____

_____

_____

_____

_____

_____

_____

_____

_____

_____

One month _____

_____

_____

_____

_____

_____

_____

_____

_____

_____

One year _____

_____

_____

_____

_____

_____

_____

_____

_____

_____

Date____/____

Today I feel deep gratitude for _____because
_____

Today I feel deep gratitude for _____because
_____

Today I feel deep gratitude for _____because
_____

Today I feel deep gratitude for _____because
_____

Today I feel deep gratitude for _____because
_____

Today my head says:
_____
_____
_____

But my heart says:
_____
_____
_____

I am completely capable of:

1_____
2_____
3_____

Future tense freewrite:

One week _____

_____

_____

_____

_____

_____

_____

_____

_____

_____

One month _____

_____

_____

_____

_____

_____

_____

_____

_____

_____

One year _____

_____

_____

_____

_____

_____

_____

_____

_____

_____

Date____/____

Today I feel deep gratitude for _____because
_____

Today I feel deep gratitude for _____because
_____

Today I feel deep gratitude for _____because
_____

Today I feel deep gratitude for _____because
_____

Today I feel deep gratitude for _____because
_____

Today my head says:
_____
_____
_____

But my heart says:
_____
_____
_____

I am completely capable of:

1_____
2_____
3_____

Future tense freewrite:

One week _____

_____

_____

_____

_____

_____

_____

_____

_____

_____

_____

One month _____

_____

_____

_____

_____

_____

_____

_____

_____

_____

_____

One year _____

_____

_____

_____

_____

_____

_____

_____

_____

_____

Date____/____

Today I feel deep gratitude for _____because
_____

Today I feel deep gratitude for _____because
_____

Today I feel deep gratitude for _____because
_____

Today I feel deep gratitude for _____because
_____

Today I feel deep gratitude for _____because
_____

Today my head says:
_____
_____
_____

But my heart says:
_____
_____
_____

I am completely capable of:

1_____
2_____
3_____

Future tense freewrite:

One week _____
_____
_____
_____
_____
_____
_____
_____
_____
_____

One month _____
_____
_____
_____
_____
_____
_____
_____
_____
_____

One year _____
_____
_____
_____
_____
_____
_____
_____
_____
_____

Date____/____

Today I feel deep gratitude for _____because
_____

Today I feel deep gratitude for _____because
_____

Today I feel deep gratitude for _____because
_____

Today I feel deep gratitude for _____because
_____

Today I feel deep gratitude for _____because
_____

Today my head says:
_____
_____
_____

But my heart says:
_____
_____
_____

I am completely capable of:

1_____
2_____
3_____

Future tense freewrite:

One week _____

_____

_____

_____

_____

_____

_____

_____

_____

_____

One month _____

_____

_____

_____

_____

_____

_____

_____

_____

_____

One year _____

_____

_____

_____

_____

_____

_____

_____

_____

_____

Date____/____

Today I feel deep gratitude for _____because
_____

Today I feel deep gratitude for _____because
_____

Today I feel deep gratitude for _____because
_____

Today I feel deep gratitude for _____because
_____

Today I feel deep gratitude for _____because
_____

Today my head says:
_____
_____
_____

But my heart says:
_____
_____
_____

I am completely capable of:

1_____
2_____
3_____

Future tense freewrite:

One week _____

_____

_____

_____

_____

_____

_____

_____

_____

_____

One month _____

_____

_____

_____

_____

_____

_____

_____

_____

_____

One year _____

_____

_____

_____

_____

_____

_____

_____

_____

_____

Date____/____

Today I feel deep gratitude for _____because
_____

Today I feel deep gratitude for _____because
_____

Today I feel deep gratitude for _____because
_____

Today I feel deep gratitude for _____because
_____

Today I feel deep gratitude for _____because
_____

Today my head says:
_____
_____
_____

But my heart says:
_____
_____
_____

I am completely capable of:

1_____
2_____
3_____

Future tense freewrite:

One week _____

_____
_____
_____
_____
_____
_____
_____
_____
_____

One month _____

_____
_____
_____
_____
_____
_____
_____
_____
_____

One year _____

_____
_____
_____
_____
_____
_____
_____
_____
_____

Date____/____

Today I feel deep gratitude for _____because
_____

Today I feel deep gratitude for _____because
_____

Today I feel deep gratitude for _____because
_____

Today I feel deep gratitude for _____because
_____

Today I feel deep gratitude for _____because
_____

Today my head says:
_____
_____
_____

But my heart says:
_____
_____
_____

I am completely capable of:

1_____
2_____
3_____

Future tense freewrite:

One week _____

_____

_____

_____

_____

_____

_____

_____

_____

_____

One month _____

_____

_____

_____

_____

_____

_____

_____

_____

_____

One year _____

_____

_____

_____

_____

_____

_____

_____

_____

_____

Date____/____

Today I feel deep gratitude for _____because
_____

Today I feel deep gratitude for _____because
_____

Today I feel deep gratitude for _____because
_____

Today I feel deep gratitude for _____because
_____

Today I feel deep gratitude for _____because
_____

Today my head says:
_____
_____
_____

But my heart says:
_____
_____
_____

I am completely capable of:

1_____
2_____
3_____

Future tense freewrite:

One week _____

_____
_____
_____
_____
_____
_____
_____
_____
_____

One month _____

_____
_____
_____
_____
_____
_____
_____
_____
_____

One year _____

_____
_____
_____
_____
_____
_____
_____
_____
_____

Date_____/_____

Today I feel deep gratitude for _____because
_____

Today I feel deep gratitude for _____because
_____

Today I feel deep gratitude for _____because
_____

Today I feel deep gratitude for _____because
_____

Today I feel deep gratitude for _____because
_____

Today my head says:
_____
_____
_____

But my heart says:
_____
_____
_____

I am completely capable of:

1_____
2_____
3_____

Future tense freewrite:

One week _____

_____

_____

_____

_____

_____

_____

_____

_____

_____

One month _____

_____

_____

_____

_____

_____

_____

_____

_____

_____

One year _____

_____

_____

_____

_____

_____

_____

_____

_____

_____

Date____/____

Today I feel deep gratitude for _____because
_____

Today I feel deep gratitude for _____because
_____

Today I feel deep gratitude for _____because
_____

Today I feel deep gratitude for _____because
_____

Today I feel deep gratitude for _____because
_____

Today my head says:
_____
_____
_____

But my heart says:
_____
_____
_____

I am completely capable of:

1_____
2_____
3_____

Future tense freewrite:

One week _____

_____

_____

_____

_____

_____

_____

_____

_____

_____

_____

One month _____

_____

_____

_____

_____

_____

_____

_____

_____

_____

_____

One year _____

_____

_____

_____

_____

_____

_____

_____

_____

_____

_____

Date____/____

Today I feel deep gratitude for _____because
_____

Today I feel deep gratitude for _____because
_____

Today I feel deep gratitude for _____because
_____

Today I feel deep gratitude for _____because
_____

Today I feel deep gratitude for _____because
_____

Today my head says:
_____
_____
_____

But my heart says:
_____
_____
_____

I am completely capable of:

1_____
2_____
3_____

Future tense freewrite:

One week _____

_____

_____

_____

_____

_____

_____

_____

_____

_____

One month _____

_____

_____

_____

_____

_____

_____

_____

_____

_____

One year _____

_____

_____

_____

_____

_____

_____

_____

_____

_____

Date____/____

Today I feel deep gratitude for _____because
_____

Today I feel deep gratitude for _____because
_____

Today I feel deep gratitude for _____because
_____

Today I feel deep gratitude for _____because
_____

Today I feel deep gratitude for _____because
_____

Today my head says:
_____
_____
_____

But my heart says:
_____
_____
_____

I am completely capable of:

1_____
2_____
3_____

Future tense freewrite:

One week _____

_____

_____

_____

_____

_____

_____

_____

_____

One month _____

_____

_____

_____

_____

_____

_____

_____

_____

One year _____

_____

_____

_____

_____

_____

_____

_____

_____

Date____/____

Today I feel deep gratitude for _____because
_____

Today I feel deep gratitude for _____because
_____

Today I feel deep gratitude for _____because
_____

Today I feel deep gratitude for _____because
_____

Today I feel deep gratitude for _____because
_____

Today my head says:
_____
_____
_____

But my heart says:
_____
_____
_____

I am completely capable of:

1_____
2_____
3_____

Future tense freewrite:

One week _____

_____
_____
_____
_____
_____
_____
_____
_____
_____

One month _____

_____
_____
_____
_____
_____
_____
_____
_____
_____

One year _____

_____
_____
_____
_____
_____
_____
_____
_____
_____

Date____/____

Today I feel deep gratitude for _____because
_____

Today I feel deep gratitude for _____because
_____

Today I feel deep gratitude for _____because
_____

Today I feel deep gratitude for _____because
_____

Today I feel deep gratitude for _____because
_____

Today my head says:
_____
_____
_____

But my heart says:
_____
_____
_____

I am completely capable of:

1_____
2_____
3_____

Future tense freewrite:

One week _____

_____

_____

_____

_____

_____

_____

_____

_____

_____

One month _____

_____

_____

_____

_____

_____

_____

_____

_____

_____

One year _____

_____

_____

_____

_____

_____

_____

_____

_____

_____

Date____/____

Today I feel deep gratitude for _____because
_____

Today I feel deep gratitude for _____because
_____

Today I feel deep gratitude for _____because
_____

Today I feel deep gratitude for _____because
_____

Today I feel deep gratitude for _____because
_____

Today my head says:
_____
_____
_____

But my heart says:
_____
_____
_____

I am completely capable of:

1_____
2_____
3_____

Future tense freewrite:

One week _____

_____
_____
_____
_____
_____
_____
_____
_____
_____
_____

One month _____

_____
_____
_____
_____
_____
_____
_____
_____
_____
_____

One year _____

_____
_____
_____
_____
_____
_____
_____
_____
_____
_____

Date____/____

Today I feel deep gratitude for _____because
_____

Today I feel deep gratitude for _____because
_____

Today I feel deep gratitude for _____because
_____

Today I feel deep gratitude for _____because
_____

Today I feel deep gratitude for _____because
_____

Today my head says:
_____
_____
_____

But my heart says:
_____
_____
_____

I am completely capable of:

1_____
2_____
3_____

Future tense freewrite:

One week _____

_____

_____

_____

_____

_____

_____

_____

_____

_____

One month _____

_____

_____

_____

_____

_____

_____

_____

_____

_____

One year _____

_____

_____

_____

_____

_____

_____

_____

_____

_____

Date____/____

Today I feel deep gratitude for _____because
_____

Today I feel deep gratitude for _____because
_____

Today I feel deep gratitude for _____because
_____

Today I feel deep gratitude for _____because
_____

Today I feel deep gratitude for _____because
_____

Today my head says:
_____
_____
_____

But my heart says:
_____
_____
_____

I am completely capable of:

1_____
2_____
3_____

Future tense freewrite:

One week _____

_____

_____

_____

_____

_____

_____

_____

_____

_____

One month _____

_____

_____

_____

_____

_____

_____

_____

_____

One year _____

_____

_____

_____

_____

_____

_____

_____

_____

Date____/____

Today I feel deep gratitude for _____because
_____

Today I feel deep gratitude for _____because
_____

Today I feel deep gratitude for _____because
_____

Today I feel deep gratitude for _____because
_____

Today I feel deep gratitude for _____because
_____

Today my head says:
_____
_____
_____

But my heart says:
_____
_____
_____

I am completely capable of:

1_____
2_____
3_____

Future tense freewrite:

One week _____
_____
_____
_____
_____
_____
_____
_____
_____
_____
_____

One month _____
_____
_____
_____
_____
_____
_____
_____
_____
_____
_____

One year _____
_____
_____
_____
_____
_____
_____
_____
_____
_____
_____

Date_____/_____

Today I feel deep gratitude for _____because
_____

Today I feel deep gratitude for _____because
_____

Today I feel deep gratitude for _____because
_____

Today I feel deep gratitude for _____because
_____

Today I feel deep gratitude for _____because
_____

Today my head says:
_____
_____
_____

But my heart says:
_____
_____
_____

I am completely capable of:

1_____
2_____
3_____

Future tense freewrite:

One week _____

_____

_____

_____

_____

_____

_____

_____

_____

_____

One month _____

_____

_____

_____

_____

_____

_____

_____

_____

_____

One year _____

_____

_____

_____

_____

_____

_____

_____

_____

_____

Date____/____

Today I feel deep gratitude for _____because
_____

Today I feel deep gratitude for _____because
_____

Today I feel deep gratitude for _____because
_____

Today I feel deep gratitude for _____because
_____

Today I feel deep gratitude for _____because
_____

Today my head says:
_____
_____
_____

But my heart says:
_____
_____
_____

I am completely capable of:

1_____
2_____
3_____

Future tense freewrite:

One week _____

_____

_____

_____

_____

_____

_____

_____

_____

_____

One month _____

_____

_____

_____

_____

_____

_____

_____

_____

_____

One year _____

_____

_____

_____

_____

_____

_____

_____

_____

_____

Date____/____

Today I feel deep gratitude for _____because
_____

Today I feel deep gratitude for _____because
_____

Today I feel deep gratitude for _____because
_____

Today I feel deep gratitude for _____because
_____

Today I feel deep gratitude for _____because
_____

Today my head says:
_____
_____
_____

But my heart says:
_____
_____
_____

I am completely capable of:

1_____
2_____
3_____

Future tense freewrite:

One week _____

_____
_____
_____
_____
_____
_____
_____
_____
_____
_____

One month _____

_____
_____
_____
_____
_____
_____
_____
_____
_____

One year _____

_____
_____
_____
_____
_____
_____
_____
_____
_____
_____

Date____/____

Today I feel deep gratitude for _____because
_____

Today I feel deep gratitude for _____because
_____

Today I feel deep gratitude for _____because
_____

Today I feel deep gratitude for _____because
_____

Today I feel deep gratitude for _____because
_____

Today my head says:
_____
_____
_____

But my heart says:
_____
_____
_____

I am completely capable of:

1_____
2_____
3_____

Future tense freewrite:

One week _____
_____
_____
_____
_____
_____
_____
_____
_____
_____

One month _____
_____
_____
_____
_____
_____
_____
_____
_____
_____

One year _____
_____
_____
_____
_____
_____
_____
_____
_____
_____

Date____/____

Today I feel deep gratitude for _____because
_____

Today I feel deep gratitude for _____because
_____

Today I feel deep gratitude for _____because
_____

Today I feel deep gratitude for _____because
_____

Today I feel deep gratitude for _____because
_____

Today my head says:
_____
_____
_____

But my heart says:
_____
_____
_____

I am completely capable of:

1_____
2_____
3_____

Future tense freewrite:

One week _____

_____

_____

_____

_____

_____

_____

_____

_____

_____

One month _____

_____

_____

_____

_____

_____

_____

_____

_____

_____

One year _____

_____

_____

_____

_____

_____

_____

_____

_____

_____

Date____/____

Today I feel deep gratitude for _____because
_____

Today I feel deep gratitude for _____because
_____

Today I feel deep gratitude for _____because
_____

Today I feel deep gratitude for _____because
_____

Today I feel deep gratitude for _____because
_____

Today my head says:
_____
_____
_____

But my heart says:
_____
_____
_____

I am completely capable of:

1_____
2_____
3_____

Future tense freewrite:

One week _____

_____

_____

_____

_____

_____

_____

_____

_____

_____

One month _____

_____

_____

_____

_____

_____

_____

_____

_____

_____

One year _____

_____

_____

_____

_____

_____

_____

_____

_____

_____

Date_____/_____

Today I feel deep gratitude for _____because
_____

Today I feel deep gratitude for _____because
_____

Today I feel deep gratitude for _____because
_____

Today I feel deep gratitude for _____because
_____

Today I feel deep gratitude for _____because
_____

Today my head says:
_____
_____
_____

But my heart says:
_____
_____
_____

I am completely capable of:

1_____
2_____
3_____

Future tense freewrite:

One week _____

_____
_____
_____
_____
_____
_____
_____
_____
_____

One month _____

_____
_____
_____
_____
_____
_____
_____
_____
_____

One year _____

_____
_____
_____
_____
_____
_____
_____
_____
_____

Date_____/_____

Today I feel deep gratitude for _____because
_____

Today I feel deep gratitude for _____because
_____

Today I feel deep gratitude for _____because
_____

Today I feel deep gratitude for _____because
_____

Today I feel deep gratitude for _____because
_____

Today my head says:
_____
_____
_____

But my heart says:
_____
_____
_____

I am completely capable of:

1_____
2_____
3_____

Future tense freewrite:

One week _____
_____
_____
_____
_____
_____
_____
_____
_____
_____

One month _____
_____
_____
_____
_____
_____
_____
_____
_____
_____

One year _____
_____
_____
_____
_____
_____
_____
_____
_____
_____

Date____/____

Today I feel deep gratitude for _____because
_____

Today I feel deep gratitude for _____because
_____

Today I feel deep gratitude for _____because
_____

Today I feel deep gratitude for _____because
_____

Today I feel deep gratitude for _____because
_____

Today my head says:
_____
_____
_____

But my heart says:
_____
_____
_____

I am completely capable of:

1_____
2_____
3_____

Future tense freewrite:

One week _____

_____

_____

_____

_____

_____

_____

_____

_____

One month _____

_____

_____

_____

_____

_____

_____

_____

_____

One year _____

_____

_____

_____

_____

_____

_____

_____

_____

_____

Date____/____

Today I feel deep gratitude for _____because
_____

Today I feel deep gratitude for _____because
_____

Today I feel deep gratitude for _____because
_____

Today I feel deep gratitude for _____because
_____

Today I feel deep gratitude for _____because
_____

Today my head says:
_____
_____
_____

But my heart says:
_____
_____
_____

I am completely capable of:

1_____
2_____
3_____

Future tense freewrite:

One week _____

_____

_____

_____

_____

_____

_____

_____

_____

_____

One month _____

_____

_____

_____

_____

_____

_____

_____

_____

One year _____

_____

_____

_____

_____

_____

_____

_____

_____

Date____/____

Today I feel deep gratitude for _____because
_____

Today I feel deep gratitude for _____because
_____

Today I feel deep gratitude for _____because
_____

Today I feel deep gratitude for _____because
_____

Today I feel deep gratitude for _____because
_____

Today my head says:
_____
_____
_____

But my heart says:
_____
_____
_____

I am completely capable of:

1_____
2_____
3_____

Future tense freewrite:

One week _____

_____

_____

_____

_____

_____

_____

_____

_____

_____

One month _____

_____

_____

_____

_____

_____

_____

_____

_____

_____

One year _____

_____

_____

_____

_____

_____

_____

_____

_____

_____

Date____/____

Today I feel deep gratitude for _____because
_____

Today I feel deep gratitude for _____because
_____

Today I feel deep gratitude for _____because
_____

Today I feel deep gratitude for _____because
_____

Today I feel deep gratitude for _____because
_____

Today my head says:
_____
_____
_____

But my heart says:
_____
_____
_____

I am completely capable of:

1_____
2_____
3_____

Future tense freewrite:

One week _____

_____
_____
_____
_____
_____
_____
_____
_____
_____

One month _____

_____
_____
_____
_____
_____
_____
_____
_____
_____

One year _____

_____
_____
_____
_____
_____
_____
_____
_____
_____

Date_____/_____

Today I feel deep gratitude for _____because
_____

Today I feel deep gratitude for _____because
_____

Today I feel deep gratitude for _____because
_____

Today I feel deep gratitude for _____because
_____

Today I feel deep gratitude for _____because
_____

Today my head says:
_____
_____
_____

But my heart says:
_____
_____
_____

I am completely capable of:

1_____
2_____
3_____

Future tense freewrite:

One week _____

_____
_____
_____
_____
_____
_____
_____
_____
_____

One month _____

_____
_____
_____
_____
_____
_____
_____
_____
_____

One year _____

_____
_____
_____
_____
_____
_____
_____
_____
_____

Date____/____

Today I feel deep gratitude for _____because
_____

Today I feel deep gratitude for _____because
_____

Today I feel deep gratitude for _____because
_____

Today I feel deep gratitude for _____because
_____

Today I feel deep gratitude for _____because
_____

Today my head says:
_____
_____
_____

But my heart says:
_____
_____
_____

I am completely capable of:

1_____
2_____
3_____

Future tense freewrite:

One week _____

_____

_____

_____

_____

_____

_____

_____

_____

One month _____

_____

_____

_____

_____

_____

_____

_____

_____

One year _____

_____

_____

_____

_____

_____

_____

_____

_____

Date____/____

Today I feel deep gratitude for _____because
_____

Today I feel deep gratitude for _____because
_____

Today I feel deep gratitude for _____because
_____

Today I feel deep gratitude for _____because
_____

Today I feel deep gratitude for _____because
_____

Today my head says:
_____
_____
_____

But my heart says:
_____
_____
_____

I am completely capable of:

1_____
2_____
3_____

Future tense freewrite:

One week _____
_____
_____
_____
_____
_____
_____
_____
_____
_____

One month _____
_____
_____
_____
_____
_____
_____
_____
_____
_____

One year _____
_____
_____
_____
_____
_____
_____
_____
_____

Date_____/_____

Today I feel deep gratitude for _____because
_____

Today I feel deep gratitude for _____because
_____

Today I feel deep gratitude for _____because
_____

Today I feel deep gratitude for _____because
_____

Today I feel deep gratitude for _____because
_____

Today my head says:
_____
_____
_____

But my heart says:
_____
_____
_____

I am completely capable of:

1_____
2_____
3_____

Future tense freewrite:

One week _____

_____

_____

_____

_____

_____

_____

_____

_____

_____

One month _____

_____

_____

_____

_____

_____

_____

_____

_____

_____

One year _____

_____

_____

_____

_____

_____

_____

_____

_____

_____

Date____/____

Today I feel deep gratitude for _____because
_____

Today I feel deep gratitude for _____because
_____

Today I feel deep gratitude for _____because
_____

Today I feel deep gratitude for _____because
_____

Today I feel deep gratitude for _____because
_____

Today my head says:
_____
_____
_____

But my heart says:
_____
_____
_____

I am completely capable of:

1_____
2_____
3_____

Future tense freewrite:

One week _____
_____
_____
_____
_____
_____
_____
_____
_____
_____

One month _____
_____
_____
_____
_____
_____
_____
_____
_____
_____

One year _____
_____
_____
_____
_____
_____
_____
_____
_____
_____

Date____/____

Today I feel deep gratitude for _____because
_____

Today I feel deep gratitude for _____because
_____

Today I feel deep gratitude for _____because
_____

Today I feel deep gratitude for _____because
_____

Today I feel deep gratitude for _____because
_____

Today my head says:
_____
_____
_____

But my heart says:
_____
_____
_____

I am completely capable of:

1_____
2_____
3_____

Future tense freewrite:

One week _____
_____
_____
_____
_____
_____
_____
_____
_____
_____

One month _____
_____
_____
_____
_____
_____
_____
_____
_____
_____

One year _____
_____
_____
_____
_____
_____
_____
_____
_____
_____

Date____/____

Today I feel deep gratitude for _____because
_____

Today I feel deep gratitude for _____because
_____

Today I feel deep gratitude for _____because
_____

Today I feel deep gratitude for _____because
_____

Today I feel deep gratitude for _____because
_____

Today my head says:
_____
_____
_____

But my heart says:
_____
_____
_____

I am completely capable of:

1_____
2_____
3_____

Future tense freewrite:

One week _____

_____

_____

_____

_____

_____

_____

_____

_____

_____

One month _____

_____

_____

_____

_____

_____

_____

_____

_____

_____

One year _____

_____

_____

_____

_____

_____

_____

_____

_____

_____

Date____/____

Today I feel deep gratitude for _____because
_____

Today I feel deep gratitude for _____because
_____

Today I feel deep gratitude for _____because
_____

Today I feel deep gratitude for _____because
_____

Today I feel deep gratitude for _____because
_____

Today my head says:
_____
_____
_____

But my heart says:
_____
_____
_____

I am completely capable of:

1_____
2_____
3_____

Future tense freewrite:

One week _____

_____

_____

_____

_____

_____

_____

_____

_____

_____

One month _____

_____

_____

_____

_____

_____

_____

_____

_____

_____

One year _____

_____

_____

_____

_____

_____

_____

_____

_____

_____

Date____/____

Today I feel deep gratitude for _____because
_____

Today I feel deep gratitude for _____because
_____

Today I feel deep gratitude for _____because
_____

Today I feel deep gratitude for _____because
_____

Today I feel deep gratitude for _____because
_____

Today my head says:
_____
_____
_____

But my heart says:
_____
_____
_____

I am completely capable of:

1_____
2_____
3_____

Future tense freewrite:

One week _____

_____

_____

_____

_____

_____

_____

_____

_____

One month _____

_____

_____

_____

_____

_____

_____

_____

_____

One year _____

_____

_____

_____

_____

_____

_____

_____

_____

Date____/____

Today I feel deep gratitude for _____because
_____

Today I feel deep gratitude for _____because
_____

Today I feel deep gratitude for _____because
_____

Today I feel deep gratitude for _____because
_____

Today I feel deep gratitude for _____because
_____

Today my head says:
_____
_____
_____

But my heart says:
_____
_____
_____

I am completely capable of:

1_____
2_____
3_____

Future tense freewrite:

One week _____

_____

_____

_____

_____

_____

_____

_____

_____

_____

One month _____

_____

_____

_____

_____

_____

_____

_____

_____

_____

One year _____

_____

_____

_____

_____

_____

_____

_____

_____

_____

Date____/____

Today I feel deep gratitude for _____because

_____

Today I feel deep gratitude for _____because

_____

Today I feel deep gratitude for _____because

_____

Today I feel deep gratitude for _____because

_____

Today I feel deep gratitude for _____because

_____

Today my head says:

_____
_____
_____

But my heart says:

_____
_____
_____

I am completely capable of:

1_____
2_____
3_____

Future tense freewrite:

One week _____

_____
_____
_____
_____
_____
_____
_____
_____
_____

One month _____

_____
_____
_____
_____
_____
_____
_____
_____
_____

One year _____

_____
_____
_____
_____
_____
_____
_____
_____
_____

Date____/____

Today I feel deep gratitude for _____because
_____

Today I feel deep gratitude for _____because
_____

Today I feel deep gratitude for _____because
_____

Today I feel deep gratitude for _____because
_____

Today I feel deep gratitude for _____because
_____

Today my head says:
_____
_____
_____

But my heart says:
_____
_____
_____

I am completely capable of:

1_____
2_____
3_____

Future tense freewrite:

One week _____

_____
_____
_____
_____
_____
_____
_____
_____
_____

One month _____

_____
_____
_____
_____
_____
_____
_____
_____
_____

One year _____

_____
_____
_____
_____
_____
_____
_____
_____
_____

Date____/____

Today I feel deep gratitude for _____because
_____

Today I feel deep gratitude for _____because
_____

Today I feel deep gratitude for _____because
_____

Today I feel deep gratitude for _____because
_____

Today I feel deep gratitude for _____because
_____

Today my head says:
_____
_____
_____

But my heart says:
_____
_____
_____

I am completely capable of:

1_____
2_____
3_____

Future tense freewrite:

One week _____

_____
_____
_____
_____
_____
_____
_____
_____
_____

One month _____

_____
_____
_____
_____
_____
_____
_____
_____
_____

One year _____

_____
_____
_____
_____
_____
_____
_____
_____
_____

Date____/____

Today I feel deep gratitude for _____because
_____

Today I feel deep gratitude for _____because
_____

Today I feel deep gratitude for _____because
_____

Today I feel deep gratitude for _____because
_____

Today I feel deep gratitude for _____because
_____

Today my head says:
_____
_____
_____

But my heart says:
_____
_____
_____

I am completely capable of:

1_____
2_____
3_____

Future tense freewrite:

One week _____

_____
_____
_____
_____
_____
_____
_____
_____
_____

One month _____

_____
_____
_____
_____
_____
_____
_____
_____
_____

One year _____

_____
_____
_____
_____
_____
_____
_____
_____
_____

Date____/____

Today I feel deep gratitude for _____because
_____

Today I feel deep gratitude for _____because
_____

Today I feel deep gratitude for _____because
_____

Today I feel deep gratitude for _____because
_____

Today I feel deep gratitude for _____because
_____

Today my head says:
_____
_____
_____

But my heart says:
_____
_____
_____

I am completely capable of:

1_____
2_____
3_____

Future tense freewrite:

One week _____

_____

_____

_____

_____

_____

_____

_____

_____

_____

One month _____

_____

_____

_____

_____

_____

_____

_____

_____

_____

One year _____

_____

_____

_____

_____

_____

_____

_____

_____

_____

Date____/____

Today I feel deep gratitude for _____because
_____

Today I feel deep gratitude for _____because
_____

Today I feel deep gratitude for _____because
_____

Today I feel deep gratitude for _____because
_____

Today I feel deep gratitude for _____because
_____

Today my head says:
_____
_____
_____

But my heart says:
_____
_____
_____

I am completely capable of:

1_____
2_____
3_____

Future tense freewrite:

One week _____

_____

_____

_____

_____

_____

_____

_____

_____

_____

One month _____

_____

_____

_____

_____

_____

_____

_____

_____

_____

One year _____

_____

_____

_____

_____

_____

_____

_____

_____

_____

Date____/____

Today I feel deep gratitude for _____because
_____

Today I feel deep gratitude for _____because
_____

Today I feel deep gratitude for _____because
_____

Today I feel deep gratitude for _____because
_____

Today I feel deep gratitude for _____because
_____

Today my head says:
_____
_____
_____

But my heart says:
_____
_____
_____

I am completely capable of:

1_____
2_____
3_____

Future tense freewrite:

One week _____

_____

_____

_____

_____

_____

_____

_____

_____

_____

One month _____

_____

_____

_____

_____

_____

_____

_____

_____

_____

One year _____

_____

_____

_____

_____

_____

_____

_____

_____

_____

Date____/____

Today I feel deep gratitude for _____because
_____

Today I feel deep gratitude for _____because
_____

Today I feel deep gratitude for _____because
_____

Today I feel deep gratitude for _____because
_____

Today I feel deep gratitude for _____because
_____

Today my head says:
_____
_____
_____

But my heart says:
_____
_____
_____

I am completely capable of:

1_____
2_____
3_____

Future tense freewrite:

One week _____

_____
_____
_____
_____
_____
_____
_____
_____
_____
_____
_____

One month _____

_____
_____
_____
_____
_____
_____
_____
_____
_____
_____
_____

One year _____

_____
_____
_____
_____
_____
_____
_____
_____
_____
_____
_____

Date____/____

Today I feel deep gratitude for _____because
_____

Today I feel deep gratitude for _____because
_____

Today I feel deep gratitude for _____because
_____

Today I feel deep gratitude for _____because
_____

Today I feel deep gratitude for _____because
_____

Today my head says:
_____
_____
_____

But my heart says:
_____
_____
_____

I am completely capable of:

1_____
2_____
3_____

Future tense freewrite:

One week _____
_____
_____
_____
_____
_____
_____
_____
_____
_____
_____

One month _____
_____
_____
_____
_____
_____
_____
_____
_____
_____
_____

One year _____
_____
_____
_____
_____
_____
_____
_____
_____
_____
_____

Date____/____

Today I feel deep gratitude for _____because
_____

Today I feel deep gratitude for _____because
_____

Today I feel deep gratitude for _____because
_____

Today I feel deep gratitude for _____because
_____

Today I feel deep gratitude for _____because
_____

Today my head says:
_____
_____
_____

But my heart says:
_____
_____
_____

I am completely capable of:

1_____
2_____
3_____

Future tense freewrite:

One week _____

_____
_____
_____
_____
_____
_____
_____
_____
_____

One month _____

_____
_____
_____
_____
_____
_____
_____
_____
_____

One year _____

_____
_____
_____
_____
_____
_____
_____
_____
_____

Date____/____

Today I feel deep gratitude for _____because
_____

Today I feel deep gratitude for _____because
_____

Today I feel deep gratitude for _____because
_____

Today I feel deep gratitude for _____because
_____

Today I feel deep gratitude for _____because
_____

Today my head says:
_____
_____
_____

But my heart says:
_____
_____
_____

I am completely capable of:

1_____
2_____
3_____

Future tense freewrite:

One week _____

_____
_____
_____
_____
_____
_____
_____
_____

One month _____

_____
_____
_____
_____
_____
_____
_____
_____

One year _____

_____
_____
_____
_____
_____
_____
_____
_____

Date____/____

Today I feel deep gratitude for _____because
_____

Today I feel deep gratitude for _____because
_____

Today I feel deep gratitude for _____because
_____

Today I feel deep gratitude for _____because
_____

Today I feel deep gratitude for _____because
_____

Today my head says:
_____
_____
_____

But my heart says:
_____
_____
_____

I am completely capable of:

1_____
2_____
3_____

Future tense freewrite:

One week _____

_____

_____

_____

_____

_____

_____

_____

_____

_____

One month _____

_____

_____

_____

_____

_____

_____

_____

_____

_____

One year _____

_____

_____

_____

_____

_____

_____

_____

_____

_____

Date____/____

Today I feel deep gratitude for _____because
_____

Today I feel deep gratitude for _____because
_____

Today I feel deep gratitude for _____because
_____

Today I feel deep gratitude for _____because
_____

Today I feel deep gratitude for _____because
_____

Today my head says:
_____
_____
_____

But my heart says:
_____
_____
_____

I am completely capable of:

1_____
2_____
3_____

Future tense freewrite:

One week _____

_____
_____
_____
_____
_____
_____
_____
_____

One month _____

_____
_____
_____
_____
_____
_____
_____
_____

One year _____

_____
_____
_____
_____
_____
_____
_____
_____

Date____/____

Today I feel deep gratitude for _____because
_____

Today I feel deep gratitude for _____because
_____

Today I feel deep gratitude for _____because
_____

Today I feel deep gratitude for _____because
_____

Today I feel deep gratitude for _____because
_____

Today my head says:
_____
_____
_____

But my heart says:
_____
_____
_____

I am completely capable of:

1_____
2_____
3_____

Future tense freewrite:

One week _____

_____

_____

_____

_____

_____

_____

_____

_____

_____

One month _____

_____

_____

_____

_____

_____

_____

_____

_____

_____

One year _____

_____

_____

_____

_____

_____

_____

_____

_____

Date____/____

Today I feel deep gratitude for _____because
_____

Today I feel deep gratitude for _____because
_____

Today I feel deep gratitude for _____because
_____

Today I feel deep gratitude for _____because
_____

Today I feel deep gratitude for _____because
_____

Today my head says:
_____
_____
_____

But my heart says:
_____
_____
_____

I am completely capable of:

1_____
2_____
3_____

Future tense freewrite:

One week _____

_____
_____
_____
_____
_____
_____
_____
_____

One month _____

_____
_____
_____
_____
_____
_____
_____
_____
_____

One year _____

_____
_____
_____
_____
_____
_____
_____
_____

Date____/____

Today I feel deep gratitude for _____because
_____

Today I feel deep gratitude for _____because
_____

Today I feel deep gratitude for _____because
_____

Today I feel deep gratitude for _____because
_____

Today I feel deep gratitude for _____because
_____

Today my head says:
_____
_____
_____

But my heart says:
_____
_____
_____

I am completely capable of:

1_____
2_____
3_____

Future tense freewrite:

One week _____
_____
_____
_____
_____
_____
_____
_____
_____

One month _____
_____
_____
_____
_____
_____
_____
_____
_____
_____
_____

One year _____
_____
_____
_____
_____
_____
_____
_____
_____
_____

Date_____/_____

Today I feel deep gratitude for _____because
_____

Today I feel deep gratitude for _____because
_____

Today I feel deep gratitude for _____because
_____

Today I feel deep gratitude for _____because
_____

Today I feel deep gratitude for _____because
_____

Today my head says:
_____
_____
_____

But my heart says:
_____
_____
_____

I am completely capable of:

1_____
2_____
3_____

Future tense freewrite:

One week _____

_____
_____
_____
_____
_____
_____
_____
_____

One month _____

_____
_____
_____
_____
_____
_____
_____
_____
_____

One year _____

_____
_____
_____
_____
_____
_____
_____
_____
_____

Date____/____

Today I feel deep gratitude for _____because
_____

Today I feel deep gratitude for _____because
_____

Today I feel deep gratitude for _____because
_____

Today I feel deep gratitude for _____because
_____

Today I feel deep gratitude for _____because
_____

Today my head says:
_____
_____
_____

But my heart says:
_____
_____
_____

I am completely capable of:

1_____
2_____
3_____

Future tense freewrite:

One week _____

_____
_____
_____
_____
_____
_____
_____
_____
_____

One month _____

_____
_____
_____
_____
_____
_____
_____
_____
_____
_____
_____

One year _____

_____
_____
_____
_____
_____
_____
_____
_____
_____
_____

Date____/____

Today I feel deep gratitude for _____because
_____

Today I feel deep gratitude for _____because
_____

Today I feel deep gratitude for _____because
_____

Today I feel deep gratitude for _____because
_____

Today I feel deep gratitude for _____because
_____

Today my head says:
_____
_____
_____

But my heart says:
_____
_____
_____

I am completely capable of:

1_____
2_____
3_____

Future tense freewrite:

One week _____

_____

_____

_____

_____

_____

_____

_____

_____

One month _____

_____

_____

_____

_____

_____

_____

_____

_____

_____

One year _____

_____

_____

_____

_____

_____

_____

_____

_____

Date____/____

Today I feel deep gratitude for _____because
_____

Today I feel deep gratitude for _____because
_____

Today I feel deep gratitude for _____because
_____

Today I feel deep gratitude for _____because
_____

Today I feel deep gratitude for _____because
_____

Today my head says:
_____
_____
_____

But my heart says:
_____
_____
_____

I am completely capable of:

1_____
2_____
3_____

Future tense freewrite:

One week _____

_____
_____
_____
_____
_____
_____
_____
_____
_____

One month _____

_____
_____
_____
_____
_____
_____
_____
_____
_____

One year _____

_____
_____
_____
_____
_____
_____
_____
_____
_____

Date____/____

Today I feel deep gratitude for _____because
_____

Today I feel deep gratitude for _____because
_____

Today I feel deep gratitude for _____because
_____

Today I feel deep gratitude for _____because
_____

Today I feel deep gratitude for _____because
_____

Today my head says:
_____
_____
_____

But my heart says:
_____
_____
_____

I am completely capable of:

1_____
2_____
3_____

Future tense freewrite:

One week _____

_____
_____
_____
_____
_____
_____
_____
_____
_____

One month _____

_____
_____
_____
_____
_____
_____
_____
_____
_____

One year _____

_____
_____
_____
_____
_____
_____
_____
_____

Date____/____

Today I feel deep gratitude for _____because
_____

Today I feel deep gratitude for _____because
_____

Today I feel deep gratitude for _____because
_____

Today I feel deep gratitude for _____because
_____

Today I feel deep gratitude for _____because
_____

Today my head says:
_____
_____
_____

But my heart says:
_____
_____
_____

I am completely capable of:

1_____
2_____
3_____

Future tense freewrite:

One week _____

_____

_____

_____

_____

_____

_____

_____

_____

One month _____

_____

_____

_____

_____

_____

_____

_____

_____

One year _____

_____

_____

_____

_____

_____

_____

_____

_____

Date_____/_____

Today I feel deep gratitude for _____because
_____

Today I feel deep gratitude for _____because
_____

Today I feel deep gratitude for _____because
_____

Today I feel deep gratitude for _____because
_____

Today I feel deep gratitude for _____because
_____

Today my head says:
_____
_____
_____

But my heart says:
_____
_____
_____

I am completely capable of:

1_____
2_____
3_____

Future tense freewrite:

One week _____

_____
_____
_____
_____
_____
_____
_____
_____
_____

One month _____

_____
_____
_____
_____
_____
_____
_____
_____
_____
_____

One year _____

_____
_____
_____
_____
_____
_____
_____
_____
_____

Date____/____

Today I feel deep gratitude for _____because
_____

Today I feel deep gratitude for _____because
_____

Today I feel deep gratitude for _____because
_____

Today I feel deep gratitude for _____because
_____

Today I feel deep gratitude for _____because
_____

Today my head says:
_____
_____
_____

But my heart says:
_____
_____
_____

I am completely capable of:

1_____
2_____
3_____

Future tense freewrite:

One week _____

_____

_____

_____

_____

_____

_____

_____

_____

One month _____

_____

_____

_____

_____

_____

_____

_____

_____

One year _____

_____

_____

_____

_____

_____

_____

_____

_____

Date_____/_____

Today I feel deep gratitude for _____because
_____

Today I feel deep gratitude for _____because
_____

Today I feel deep gratitude for _____because
_____

Today I feel deep gratitude for _____because
_____

Today I feel deep gratitude for _____because
_____

Today my head says:
_____
_____
_____

But my heart says:
_____
_____
_____

I am completely capable of:

1_____
2_____
3_____

Future tense freewrite:

One week _____

_____
_____
_____
_____
_____
_____
_____
_____

One month _____

_____
_____
_____
_____
_____
_____
_____
_____

One year _____

_____
_____
_____
_____
_____
_____
_____
_____

Date_____/_____

Today I feel deep gratitude for _____because
_____

Today I feel deep gratitude for _____because
_____

Today I feel deep gratitude for _____because
_____

Today I feel deep gratitude for _____because
_____

Today I feel deep gratitude for _____because
_____

Today my head says:
_____
_____
_____

But my heart says:
_____
_____
_____

I am completely capable of:

1_____
2_____
3_____

Future tense freewrite:

One week _____
_____
_____
_____
_____
_____
_____
_____
_____

One month _____
_____
_____
_____
_____
_____
_____
_____
_____

One year _____
_____
_____
_____
_____
_____
_____
_____
_____
_____

Date____/____

Today I feel deep gratitude for _____because
_____

Today I feel deep gratitude for _____because
_____

Today I feel deep gratitude for _____because
_____

Today I feel deep gratitude for _____because
_____

Today I feel deep gratitude for _____because
_____

Today my head says:
_____
_____
_____

But my heart says:
_____
_____
_____

I am completely capable of:

1_____
2_____
3_____

Future tense freewrite:

One week _____

_____

_____

_____

_____

_____

_____

_____

_____

_____

One month _____

_____

_____

_____

_____

_____

_____

_____

_____

_____

One year _____

_____

_____

_____

_____

_____

_____

_____

_____

_____

Date_____/_____

Today I feel deep gratitude for _____because
_____

Today I feel deep gratitude for _____because
_____

Today I feel deep gratitude for _____because
_____

Today I feel deep gratitude for _____because
_____

Today I feel deep gratitude for _____because
_____

Today my head says:
_____
_____
_____

But my heart says:
_____
_____
_____

I am completely capable of:

1_____
2_____
3_____

Future tense freewrite:

One week _____

_____

_____

_____

_____

_____

_____

_____

_____

One month _____

_____

_____

_____

_____

_____

_____

_____

_____

One year _____

_____

_____

_____

_____

_____

_____

_____

_____

Date____/____

Today I feel deep gratitude for _____because
_____

Today I feel deep gratitude for _____because
_____

Today I feel deep gratitude for _____because
_____

Today I feel deep gratitude for _____because
_____

Today I feel deep gratitude for _____because
_____

Today my head says:
_____
_____
_____

But my heart says:
_____
_____
_____

I am completely capable of:

1_____
2_____
3_____

Future tense freewrite:

One week _____

_____

_____

_____

_____

_____

_____

_____

_____

_____

One month _____

_____

_____

_____

_____

_____

_____

_____

_____

_____

_____

One year _____

_____

_____

_____

_____

_____

_____

_____

_____

_____